W9-BSL-319

Backyard Books

Are you a Bee?

KINGFISHER
Larousse Kingfisher Chambers Inc.
95 Madison Avenue
New York, New York 10016

First published in 2000

1 3 5 7 9 10 8 6 4 2

1TR/1100/TWP/DIG/150NYMA

LIBRARY OF CONGRESS CATALOGING-IN-PUBLICATION DATA
has been applied for.

ISBN 0-7534-5345-2

Editors: Katie Puckett, Carron Brown
Series Designers: Jane Tassie, Jane Buckley

Printed in Singapore

Are You a Bee?

Judy Allen and Tudor Humphries

KING*f*ISHER

NEW YORK

Are you a bee?

Perhaps you are a honeybee.
If so, your mother is a queen.
She looks like this, and she
lays eggs.

Your life began inside
one of her eggs.

When you hatch, you are not
a pretty sight.

You are a larva.

You are in a small room with
six walls. It's called a cell.

Your older sisters bring food.
Eat it and grow.

Grow until you fill your cell.

One of your older sisters puts
a wax ceiling on your cell.

Inside your closed cell you change a lot.

When you are ready, chew a hole in the ceiling and climb out.

NOW you look like a bee.

You have a hairy body with stripes,
six legs, and four wings.
You have two feelers on your head.
You have a stinger.

You are not alone. You have
a few hundred brothers and
thousands of sisters.

You live in a nest built by
your older sisters.

Your nest might be in
a hollow tree.

It might hang down from
a tree branch.

Most likely it will
be inside a hive.

Your brothers
are drones.
They don't do much.

You and your sisters
are workers.
You do everything.

You clean the nest,
feed the larvae, take care of
the queen, and build new cells.

You fan the nest
with your wings to
cool it in the summer.

You guard the nest to keep
out strange bees.

Busy, busy, busy.

Leave the nest to
fetch food from flowers.

How will you know
where to look?

Your sisters will
make up a dance to tell you.

Watch the dance carefully.
Don't worry, you'll understand it—

you're a bee.

There is sweet liquid
in flowers. It's called
nectar, and it's hidden
deep inside. This is not
a problem. You have
a long tongue.
You
can
reach it.

You also have a special
stomach to carry it in.
You'll get pollen-dust all
over you. Scrape it off with
your front legs and put
it in the pollen baskets
on your
back legs.

When you get home,
your sisters will help
you put the nectar and
the pollen into storage
cells. Mix some of the
nectar with pollen
to make beebread.

Leave the rest of the
nectar to turn into honey.

Beebread is good to eat.
So is honey.

If you find a new patch
of flowers, be sure to tell
your sisters.

How?
Dance, of course!

More eggs hatch.
More larvae turn into bees.
The nest gets very crowded.
What will happen next?

The old queen,
your mother, leaves.

She takes you and a lot
of your sisters with her.

Deep in the nest a royal larva is hatching. She is in a different kind of cell, and she is fed rich food called royal jelly. When she becomes a bee, she is a young queen.

She flies away and mates with drones from another nest so that she can lay eggs. When she flies home again, she will be the new queen.

21

Fly with your sisters—follow
the old queen.

Stay together—you are part of a swarm.
When the queen stops,
swarm around her.

Now you must build a new
nest. But where?

Maybe the queen will send
scout bees to find a good place.

Or maybe a beekeeper will find you and take you all to an empty hive.

Why is the beekeeper dressed like this?

In case you get flustered and try to sting.

However,

if your mother looks
a little like this   or this

or this

you are not a bee.

You are...

25

...a human child.

You do not have a hairy body
with stripes on it.

You do not have a long tongue.

You do not have a stinger.

It is very unlikely that you have hundreds of brothers and thousands of sisters.

But you can do a lot
of things that a bee can't do.

You can still eat bread and honey,
but you'll never have to fetch
your food from flowers.

Best of all,
you don't have
to be busy, busy,
busy all day long.

Did You Know...

...bees are happy to live in a hive, because the beekeeper has already built part of the nest for them. If bees live in a hollow tree, they have to build the whole nest themselves.

...a worker bee can sting only once, then it dies—but a queen bee can sting many times.

...bees carry pollen from flower to flower on their furry bodies. The pollen from one flower rubs off onto others and makes seeds, which will grow into new plants.

...the average worker bee makes one-and-a-half teaspoons of honey in her lifetime.